# NO STRANGE LAND

Meditations and Prayers
by
Eddie Askew

By the same author:
A Silence and A Shouting
Disguises of Love
Many Voices One Voice
Facing the Storm

©The Leprosy Mission International
80 Windmill Road, Brentford
Middlesex TW8 0QH, UK
1987
2nd Impression 1990

ISBN 0 902731 26 2

Photoset and printed by Stanley L. Hunt (Printers) Ltd, Rushden, Northants

To my mother,
a strong supporter
from earliest days.
With love.


Cover picture: Loch Etive, Scotland — from a pastel painting by the author

# Foreword

A PPRECIATIVE and often very moving comments testify the way in which God has used Eddie Askew's first three collections of meditations and prayers. In this fourth volume, the author's humanity, integrity and artistry once more emerge, as he adds prayers and pencil drawings to thoughts from his monthly newsletter to Leprosy Mission colleagues worldwide.

No Strange Land is published as Eddie Askew retires from the post of International Director of The Leprosy Mission, which he has held since 1974. Previously, he and his wife Barbara spent 15 years working with the Mission in India.

COUNTRY LANE, SUSSEX

# Psalm 137

BEWILDERED Jewish exiles, far away in Babylon, were weary and deeply homesick. Jerusalem was a distant dream, the daily reality was harsh and alien. They wept as they remembered their country. Their feelings had been trampled on by insensitive captors. They felt abandoned. Looking back towards home, longing to return, the psalm writer crystallises their feelings in a passionate poem of despair and anger. Read it in Psalm 137.

Overwhelmed by despair, they can't even worship. "How could we sing the Lord's song in a strange land?" he asks.

Part of the problem was a misunderstanding of the nature of their God. In common with other nations of their time, they saw God as a national figure, someone whose presence and power was somehow limited to his own territory. They found it hard to "sing the Lord's song" because they thought he was far away, thought themselves abandoned, alone and helpless.

It's easy to feel that way when trouble strikes. We wall ourselves in behind our misery and, because our vision has so narrowed, we can't see or feel God's presence. But he is still there, and he still cares. We may feel estranged and lost, in a place we don't know, but take comfort. There is no strange land to God. Everywhere is home. His love, compassion and healing are at work wherever we are. Reach out and he is there.

Lord, it's so easy to give in.
To let the clouds gather
dark and threatening,
whipped up by the winds of my own fear.
Mists of my own making
blotting out the light and warmth of your presence.
So easy, in mouth-dry anxiety,
to feel alone.
Abandoned. Unprotected.

To roll in nettlebeds of self-pity,
the pain spreading as vision contracts,
until my horizon is described
by the jangled nerve endings of my despair.

Estranged. Alien.
Each accustomed act, new,
unknown, frightening.

And yet, Lord, you are near.
I hold on to your promise
"For I am with you, always."
Always. Unconditional.
Words echoing
through the deep caverns of my doubt,
sometimes distant, sometimes near.
I reach out
feeling in the dark for reassurance.
And we meet. Touch.
Your hand held out too. First.
I hold on, warming my cold, fearful fingers
in the glow of your presence.
I hear your voice,
speaking my language.
Words I understand.
And I realise
there are no strange lands to you.
Your presence everywhere.
Your presence, home.
Thank you.

# Psalm 148

I'M sitting at a window in Thimpu, the capital of Bhutan. It's early morning, the air still crisp under a blue sky. Tentative fingers of sunshine stroke the near hills, promising later warmth. Light touches the far mountains. Travelling in Bhutan makes you very conscious of the immensity and power of creation. The enormous forces which thrust up the towering Himalayas, the rush of glacial rivers, moulding smooth the jagged rocks. The continuing processes of growth, erosion still changing the structure and face of the land. Yet these forces of creation are not an end in themselves. They are simply the tools used by God the creator, and the creator is greater than the tools he uses.

Yesterday, we gathered in a small room at a leprosy hospital for a morning communion service. There were about forty of us, of different nationalities, backgrounds and skills. We read Psalm 148 — a poem of praise to the creator, the words brought alive by the surroundings. And there we were, ordinary human beings, tapping into the resources and power of this God; the resources of a God who is always with us.

A few days earlier, I'd been in Darjeeling. There, on a clear day, you can see the breathtaking snow peaks of Kanchenjunga, towering and beautiful. Some days, though, the clouds boil up from the plains below, masking the view. You look out onto grey mist, and it's hard to realize the mountains are still there. But they are. In spite of the mist, they remain just as close, just as real.

So is the presence and power of God. Whether we feel him close, or distanced by our human fallibility, misted by our worries, he is there. His power and love ready to be experienced, lived in, celebrated.

I praise you.
Lord of creation.
You spoke the word, and all things came to be.
Lord of life.
You speak the word, and all creation lives.
Echoes and shouts with life.
Your life.

No static world,
where everything is set in place and nothing moves.
No ancient pile of stones, inert, cathedral quiet,
dozing with old memories, days done.
But full of life, trembling in intensity.
Vibrant as quartz crystal.
Dynamic with your energy.
Power, elemental and profound.
I stand in awe.
All I can do is take my little part
in praise with all creation.

Praise and rejoice
that this deep power that I call Lord
is crystallised in love.
Made personal and close.
The thunder of the universe articulate in quiet voice,
gentle to my ear.
Holding itself in readiness
to meet my needs.
Lord of the universe, who bends to me.
Creator to created.
Infinite to infinitesimal.
What can I do but praise?

And yet Lord, pressed by my own busyness
and self-created doubts,
I lose my grip on you.
The clouds draw in and shadow me.
The mist wet-blankets me in billows of uncertainty.
My doubt shouts out for reassurance
and comes echoing back, empty handed.
Yet still you're there.

Your presence patient and dependable.
And in its magnet field
I turn again to find you.
True north
by which I orientate my life.

And praise returns.

HINDSWEPT TREES, CUMBRIA

# Luke 2:8-18

A COLLEAGUE drew my attention to a poem I'd never seen before. It begins:

> "Blessed art Thou, O Christmas Christ,
> that Thy cradle was so low that shepherds,
> poorest and simplest of all earthly folk,
> could yet kneel beside it,
> and look level-eyed into the face of God."

What an amazing image. "Look level-eyed into the face of God." I imagine the shepherds perhaps visiting Jerusalem one year for Passover, although the Bible doesn't say they were Jews, just shepherds. And the Angels told them the good news was for *all* people. But I see them struggling through the crowds in the bazaar, past the money-changing tables (did they accept Aramaic Express cards?), to the temple. Overawed by the robes, the ritual, and the architecture, maybe they'd feel God's power and magnificence, but would they feel his love?

Turn to the baby. A down-to-earth event in more than one sense. God found in human form, to touch, to see, to live with, near at hand. The shepherds come and kneel, and look level-eyed into his face. The poor look at the poor and see God. One thing to note. They had to kneel to look. Humility meets humility and discovers God. And it's in worship that we meet him, too.

There's another dimension as well, there always is. The thing that makes me look down, avoid another's gaze, is embarrassment or shame. That's gone. The baby, grown to manhood, stretched to his limit on the cross, has taken the shame. He encourages, and enables, me to look straight, level-eyed, into his face.

A final word, if anything is final. The image has another implication. We most often look level-eyed into the faces of those around us — workmates, family, neighbours. God's in them too. That's where we find him, looking level-eyed at us. And that includes the lonely, the dispossessed, the sick and hungry. That's where he is.

Lord, why a stable?
With its dirt, and poverty, and smell.
The need to step with care in the straw.
I could have understood a palace.
Much more fitting for a king. God's son.

Or at least a good middleclass home.
Where everyone knows the right values,
goes to the right school, holds solid opinions.
The sort of background that makes leaders.

But not for you.
The people in your home had dirt under their finger nails.
A sign of honest work, but nothing influential.

And yet your coming broke the barriers.
Not through the slow erosion of wave on rock,
but in a quick, star-streaming, blazing burst of love.
Brought God to man.
Love levelling the differences.

To see you, to gaze into your eyes,
no need to reach, climb upwards,
or stretch on superspiritual tiptoe.
Simply to kneel,
the only casualty my pride.
It makes me want to argue, Lord,
and ask was there no other way?
But logic loses out to love.
And logic, anyway, would say
that I could never reach you on my own.

The great thing is that your demands
you first made on yourself.
I see you, when I kneel, because you knelt first.
And when I kneel, defences down,
your hands reach out and, suddenly,
I'm standing on my feet again,
and see you looking out from every face.

## Matthew 7:7-13

I 'VE been thinking about travel. After all, I do a lot of it. I was reading an assessment of C. G. Jung, the pioneer psychologist. At one point Jung commented on the growing fashion for tourist travel. He could accept travel for work's sake, but constant travel for travel's sake made him wonder. What inward journey was the traveller running away from? Was he substituting his exploration of new lands for the need to explore the mountains and deep valleys of his own personality? Was he running from himself, and from God, to get lost in a relatively safe external world?

Don't cancel your annual trip to Spain or wherever, Jung was talking about those who are no sooner home than out again. And again. We all need to travel, to stretch the cords that bind us too tightly to the background and attitudes we've grown up with. To loosen our dependence on the known and comfortable. To open us to new learning. The Prodigal Son did it, taking his money and disappearing over the horizon. For him, it was a spiritual journey too, a time of testing. Something we must all do unless we're content to live as adolescents. In testing his own values and beliefs, the prodigal came to understand how inadequate they were, how soon burnt out, and how dry the ashes could taste.

In the end, he returned to his beginning, back to the family. (Incidentally, I wish his mother had been mentioned in the welcome. Maybe she was taken for granted, as women often are, cooking the fatted calf.) The son came back threadbare, but with a new understanding of himself, his relationships, and his place in the world. T. S. Eliot, wrote that each of us is ". . . outward bound only in order to return . . . the inward way from where we started, and to see the place for the first time".

"To see the place for the first time." Travel often opens our eyes to the beauties of where we began. The spiritual journey helps us see our beginnings with new eyes of wonder. We travel to find ourselves; we return to find God at the starting point. And in the joy of finding him we ask "Why did I ever leave?" But we wouldn't have found him if we hadn't left, we wouldn't know the wonder of his love. On the journey we come to see our own poverty, the riches he shares with us, and where home really is.

A great adventure, Lord.
I sense the excitement in his mind.
The prodigal, taking all he had,
and moving out.
A feeling of freedom in the air.
Stretching the strings that held him back.
Rejecting home,
familiar, undervalued,
and stepping out into the world.

I too have seen the sights.
Blown my mind with new experiences.
Grabbed them with both hands,
wringing each reluctant drop from life.

Yet every new excitement something less.
And behind the highs lies doubt.
The courage I wear coming apart at the seams.
Until I stand,
dry-mouthed in disillusion.
Even the dregs as dry as dust.
Living an emptiness.
The wind of loneliness
blowing sand in my eyes.
Painful. The road a blur.

I turn for home.
Not with the joy of journey's end
as guiding star,
but in night-dark despair.
Reluctantly.
But in the coming back
I find the love I searched for.
The strings that bound me, burdensome,
are, in reality, safe anchors.
Holding me tight in love,
not slavery.
I see you new,
and realise
my end in my beginning.
Beginning and end,
in you.

# Matthew 6:28-34

JOSEPH MALLARD WILLIAM TURNER was one of Britain's master painters. He had to be something special, with a name like that. In earlier days, people most admired his large, highly finished oil paintings. Today, tastes are different, and many people prefer his small watercolours.

I've just bought a book of his watercolours of Venice. Painted around 1819-1840, many of them have never been published before. They are breathtaking. Full of light and atmosphere, and colour. But when you look carefully, the pictures surprise you. Many of them are a simple running together of colour, blue-greys, soft reds, pale yellows.

Turner painted them wet, letting the colours flow into each other. There are few clear edges, or defined shapes. Then, when the paint was dry, Turner would take a little stronger colour on his brush or pen. With a few crisp, confident strokes, the blur became a picture, the background colours given meaning and definition.

It doesn't happen by accident. A good watercolour, and these are far better than "good", is planned right from the start. The earlier, less defined, areas are all part of the process.

There are times when life seems undefined, ragged. Times when all we can do is get on with the routine, without any clear sense of direction or purpose. Then some event, some word, draws it all together. We see what it was leading up to, and it makes sense. There was no need for concern. God paints in a few crisp strokes that give meaning to the whole.

But that's not quite right. It's not just the final strokes of the brush that are God's. The preparatory painting is his too. The colours laid down, apparently at random, are just as much part of the complete painting. He could produce the meticulous detail of the oil painting everytime, but the choice is his. And whichever way he does it, the result is masterly.

Lord, sometimes I get worried.
Uptight.
My life seems blurred,
ragged at the edges,
the definition poor, unfocused.
I feel uncomfortable. Unsure.
Nothing clear cut, decisive.
No white lines along the middle of the road
to lead me through the bend.
And when I'm round the corner,
there's still another bend ahead.
The road's not easy to see, the signposts few.

At times like this, Lord,
set my mind on you.
Help me to frame my life firmly,
and leave it in your hands.
Content to watch the colours ebb and flow.

Sometimes the clear bright shining
sparkles with light.
Dazzles the eyes.
But then the muted greys,
deep darks, flood in.
As integral a part of your harmonies
as all the rest.
Then let me see your beauty
even in the shadows.
And when the time is right,
your time, not mine,
I hope to see your finger,
creative still,
trace out, in lines of love,
the purposes you had in mind
from the beginning.

# Luke 9:23-26

TWO hundred years ago, in Japan, lived a famous painter named Hokusai. A patron came to see him. He asked for a painting of a cockerel in all its glory. Hokusai agreed. Sometime later, the patron sent a servant, asking if the painting was ready. "Not yet," said the painter. Again, after some time, the same thing happened. A year went by and then the rich patron came himself. "Is my painting still not ready?" he asked. The painter took him into his studio. He stretched a piece of silk, prepared his paints and brushes and, in a few minutes, produced a magnificent painting. His patron was overjoyed, but then began to get angry. "If you could paint that picture in ten minutes," he asked, "why have you kept me waiting so long for it?" Hokusai led him into the next room. There, all over the floor, were stacks of drawings, sketches, studies of cockerels. Some of the whole bird, others of a head, or a claw, or a feather. The reason he could paint the ten-minute masterpiece was the year's work he had spent in preparation.

There are no short cuts, either in painting or the Christian life.

Jesus said, "If anyone wishes to be a follower of mine, he must leave self behind; day after day he must take up his cross, and come with me . . ." (Luke 9:23).

Day after day. It's not the short burst of enthusiasm, quickly spent, that achieves results, but the disciplined living of daily life, the willing acceptance of hard work and routine, taken and carried out faithfully and continually.

A painter-friend of mine says that to keep his skill he must draw or paint something every day. If he doesn't, the accuracy and coordination are a little less than they should be. And it happens to the Christian too. Discipleship is discipline, but sweetened with love. His love, not ours. As freely given as he took up the cross in the first place. And with the love comes the strength to carry the cross, each day.

*Day after day.*
*That sobers me up. Lord.*
*It dissipates the nice warm feeling of commitment,*
*like new wine sipped,*
*light on the tongue and fresh.*
*Cold-showered in the reality of your word.*

*Day after day?*
*I can handle a bright burst of new enthusiasm,*
*short lived as spring sunshine.*
*It fits my diary.*
*I'm free on Tuesday, seven to ten.*
*Or Sunday afternoon.*
*And when it's over*
*I can move to something else.*

*Day after day,*
*The long grind in low gear*
*up the steep hill of daily living, daily giving.*
*The sharp corners, hairpin bends,*
*the sudden dips, the concentration,*
*tiring mind and muscle.*
*I grab the map and look for easier ways,*
*for moral motorways that speed the journey on.*
*Short cuts to bypass all the hassle.*
*They're not marked.*

*Day after day.*
*The only way.*
*Then suddenly the realisation comes.*
*Your presence with me. Quietly, consistently.*
*Yours too the daily walk,*
*the patient taking of the narrow road.*
*The constancy.*
*The faithful sharing of the burden.*
*And when, reluctantly and wondering,*
*I ask, "Day after day?"*
*I see you nod and say,*
*"I'm with you. Day after day."*

*Let's make a start, Lord.*

# Micah 6:1-8

WHEN Micah the prophet began to tear strips off his people for their bad behaviour they turned to the traditional — animal sacrifice, burning oil on the altars, even offering their children. In passing, have you noticed how much easier it is to sacrifice other people, rather than one's self? A British politician's actions were once described as "Greater love hath no man than this, that a man lay down his friends for his life!" Micah wouldn't let his people get away with that. He asked, ". . . and what is it that the Lord asks of you? Only to act justly, to love mercy, and to walk humbly with your God" (Micah 6:6-8). Micah asserts that God demands not tokens, but radically changed lifestyle.

Are his words relevant now? We're often ready to "sacrifice", to please God and prove our commitment. What are our sacrifices? Maybe a punishing work schedule, scurrying round brandishing a full diary. Some of us pretend to dislike it, but it does wonders for the ego! We don't sacrifice our firstborn, or do we? I've known Christians who've neglected their families for "the work". Criticism is countered by saying, "What else can I do? It's the only thing possible." We substitute the "possible" — work, for a change in lifestyle — the "impossible".

Claude Monet's later paintings are a shimmer of light. They vibrate and flow; shapes dissolve in living colour. He ·was a great master of Impressionism, and yet he was never satisfied with what he'd done. "If only I could be content with the possible," he once sighed, as he struggled over another painting.

We're too often content with the possible. We hide behind the "sacrifice", even though we know God really wants ourselves, our egos. True sacrifice involves respecting the rights and living space of others. Taking no more than our fair share, or less — justice. Accepting others in love, substituting understanding for prejudice — mercy. It's tough. And as for walking humbly — well that really is going over the top. Isn't it just a bit too much to expect, Lord? Micah didn't think so.

Lord, what do you want?
Another hour at work?
A bit more in the collection plate?
A smile, a cheque
when the Oxfam man comes round?
I reckon I can manage that,
if it's clear that's what you ask.
And in the giving I'll get a bonus too.
I'll feel good, having made the effort.
Feel more than good, as I stand
warming my hands at the fire of self-satisfaction.

Can we leave it that way, Lord?
I'll do my bit and you'll do yours.
My little world secure, unshaken.
The even progress of my life
undisturbed by earth tremors of real commitment.
Many do less.

But as I'm tempted to relax,
I feel uneasy.
I'm only playing games.
Hiding the face of my selfishness
behind gestures of goodwill.
Counting to a hundred and hoping I'll not be found.

Your words cut deep.
Slice through the skin of my hypocrisy.
Lay bare the truth inside.
Your loving hands reach down to take,
not the small things I offer
in the hope they'll be enough,
but me. No less.
My world rocks in the earthquake of your approach,
the impossibility of your demands.
But as I let go, surrender,
I find a new stability,
as I stand, hands empty, in your presence.
Your love seeps in through the cracks in my ego.
Fills the empty spaces with your grace.

# Luke 22:39-46

THERE were no neat lawns, no formal flower beds in Gethsemane's garden. There were olive trees scattered over the hillside — Gethsemane means "oil press" — and straggly grass and dust. A place of peace and quiet away from the city, except when the olives were harvested. I guess Jesus was attracted by the quiet.

It was quiet the last time he went there, at night, but the peace had gone. It was a time of tension: Jesus struggling with himself, striving with God. Somehow, it's easy to get smug, gloss over the struggle, and concentrate on Jesus' decision. "Yet not my will, but thine be done" (Luke 22:42). Nice and easy. "Ah," we say, "He always did his father's will." True, but there was nothing easy about it. Look at the struggle.

It echoes our own struggles. The constant battle of our will versus God's. The fight to go our own way, not his. We'll do anything to avoid it, argue, pretend, rationalise. Yet if we were to put less energy into fighting, there'd be more left to do the work! We screw ourselves up so tightly raising objections that we've nothing left over for constructive thought. But from the cross Jesus offers us a new freedom. In his powerful book *Celebration of Discipline*, Richard Foster describes it as "the ability to lay down the terrible burden of always needing to get your own way". Obedience — a free decision we make towards God — leads to a freedom from self. Something worth fighting for.

And when you look at it more closely, the struggle isn't really against God, but against self, and God is actually fighting on our side, if only we let him.

It's some battle, Lord.
I've been fighting it since the day I was born.
Fighting for my own way.
Pegging out my own boundaries.
Strengthening my own laager.
Loading the guns
and shooting hard and fast
at the first, faint tremblings
of approaching danger.

I'm not an ego-maniac,
I just want my own way!

It's funny, Lord. The cosmic joke.
Here I am, cowering yet aggressive,
defending my little patch of jungle.
The wire rolled out and pinned,
paths mined and booby-trapped,
while you are offering me
free access to the world.
I'm all blind fury, snapping at thin air.
And all I do is jar my teeth
and bite my tongue.

I'm tired of fighting, Lord.
It never seems to end.
One skirmish hardly over,
the vanguard of the next comes
creeping through the trees,
its movement brushing the branches
of my entangled fears.

Peace, Lord, peace.
And as I sink back, hurting,
expecting you to ride roughshod,
victor over vanquished,
I look through tired eyes
and see you by my side.
Friend not foe.
Fighting with me, not against.
And out there in the pitted landscape of my war
the only casualty is self.

*I struggle upright, stand again in new freedom*
*and, for the first time,*
*I can look into your eyes,*
*without reserve.*

GLOUCESTERSHIRE FARM

# Matthew 5:43-48

NO matter how hard you try, how carefully you word what you say or write, things get misunderstood. Your motives may be the best, but motives can't be seen or touched. Only the word is there to be taken and, sometimes, misinterpreted. And if there's one thing we humans are good at, it's misunderstanding. There's a deep insecurity in each of us that makes us so sensitive to attack that we see danger where it doesn't exist. Then, in response to the mirage, we defend ourselves, attack without reason, saddle someone with motives he'd never thought of, and hurt him unjustly.

It happened to Jesus, and he warned that it would happen to his followers. But Jesus used the problem creatively. He didn't say simply, "Watch out! Follow me and you're in for trouble." He said, "Blessed are you when people insult you, persecute you, and falsely say all manner of evil against you . . ." (Matt. 5:11).

I think though, that it's a verse you have to keep in context. It's part of the Sermon on the Mount, and follows Jesus's comments on the character and behaviour his disciples should struggle for. And it is a struggle. The whole passage suggests to me that the blessing comes, not in the simple fact of being wrongly accused (how blessed I'd be!), but in the response I make to it. Look through those earlier verses and note some of the words — meek, merciful, peacemaker. There's nothing about hitting back, however hard I look.

The problem about retaliation is where it ends. Someone said that the doctrine of an eye for an eye would lead to universal blindness. At some point, and the sooner the better, we have to break the chain. Refuse to be provoked. Take the stones thrown at us and, instead of throwing them back, use them to build another small corner of God's kingdom. It's tough, it hurts, we need to grab hold of every bit of love we can reach, but I believe it can be done. May the Lord give us the grace to do it. And maybe, too, we need the grace to look honestly at our motives to check they are the best!

Lord, it can be hard work, sometimes,
holding on to you.
There are rough moments
when people I've believed in, worked with,
seem to change.
When misunderstanding and hurt feelings
wield words like whips,
cutting across the taut and tender flesh
of our relationship.
Opening deep wounds that hurt and bleed.
And when the bleeding stops, the pain remains.
And as the pain dies slowly, the scar lies livid,
an unwanted memory of things I'd willingly forget.

I try, but some chance thought triggers instant recall,
and I rehearse it all again,
call up the file, and watch it spread,
electron-quick, across the screen of memory.
Misery in megabytes.

And then I see you in the shadow,
stretched beyond bearing on the cross.
Lord, it's tempting, but let me not compare
the little hurts and scratches of my life
with yours.
To call my hurts a crucifixion is exaggeration.
Enlarged beyond reality.
Dramatised beyond truth.
But still it hurts,
and in the aching moment
I need your arms around me.

And as your hands reach out
I see the scars and, just a little,
I begin to feel what you went through for me.
I take the ache and pain
and offer it to you.
Protest no more,
just wait, and wait,
and try to love again.

*But, Lord, it's hard.*
*Your grace may be sufficient,*
*but only just!*

FAMILY PICNIC, RICHMOND PARK

## Matthew 6:31-34

OVER Christmas, a friend said something that made me look at the nativity story with new eyes. Usually, when we look at it, it's with all the information we've inherited. All we know about Jesus's life and death, and resurrection. We interpret it through nearly two thousand years of theology and church life.

But Mary and Joseph had none of that. They knew their baby was special in some way. The visits of the shepherds and wise men pointed to that, but it wasn't very clear. The vision they'd had told them to name him Jesus. It meant "saviour", but it was a common name. Even being told that he'd save people from their sins wasn't very explicit, seen from where they were.

It was made harder by other events. Mary and Joseph weren't in control of their lives. They'd been compelled to go to Bethlehem for a census, on Roman orders. Then, King Herod's soldiers got in the way, and they had to run for safety to Egypt as refugees.

Looking at later events, I'm sure it was a blessing that they didn't know in detail what life held for them all, especially about the baby's call to preach and die.

There are times when we wish we knew more about the future. Moments when we'd like to feel in better control of life, but we can't. Life's not like that. Each day we walk into the unknown as Mary and Joseph did. And, like them, we find strength for that one day. And then the next.

We have one advantage though, that they didn't have. We do know who Jesus is, and what he's done. And we have the confidence of walking into each day with him.

It's easy talking, Lord,
about not being anxious.
Taking each day as it comes.
"No point in worrying," they say.
I'm not so sure of that,
the things I worry about don't usually happen!

I look at Joseph,
and his responsibilities.
A wife. New baby.
Away from home, and pushed further
by forces he couldn't control.
Did he have the same moments of panic
that I have?
Bleak moments,
when it seems that nothing I know
will help me through the day.
And I'm running scared, tail down,
ready to jump in the nearest hole.

Sometimes, Lord,
I wish you'd tell me more.
Prepare me.
Whisper in my ear
a weather forecast of a sunnier day tomorrow.
Or warn me of the storm to come,
so I could grab a spiritual umbrella
and stay dry.

But then I realise
I know all I need to know.
And that's the fact
that you know all my needs.
And, wet or dry,
in calm or storm,
you're in it with me.
And that's enough.
Just for today.

# Psalm 104:19-35

I 'VE a new toy, a bio-clock. I'm not talking about that inner feeling that tells me when it's lunchtime, or makes me sleepy at night; that's quite different. This is a small quartz clock. There are no batteries. It runs on Coca-cola, or an apple, or most other fruit. No, I'm not joking. The wires from the clock end in bits of metal, one copper, the other zinc. Push these into an apple, or dangle them in the Coca-cola tin, and the clock begins to work.

More than a hundred and fifty years ago, a man named Volta discovered that if bits of different metals are immersed in a weak acid an electric current is generated between them. He called it a Voltaic battery. Both the apple and the coke are acidic, and produce enough electricity for the clock. So far it's worked for three months non-stop, although the apple is getting a bit brown and wizened, and may soon need changing.

I'm fascinated by the thought of all the power latent in the world around us. Energy, waiting to be discovered, released, and used, in ways which would have seemed miraculous in other days, but which we take for granted. All part of God's creation. All conforming to what we call "natural laws", but which we can't explain away just by describing and naming them.

The psalmist looks at God's world and is awed: "Countless are the things thou hast made, O Lord. Thou hast made all by thy wisdom" (Psalm 104:24). We've added to our scientific knowledge since his day, but we've lost the sense of reverence when faced with the marvellous intricacies of the world. And still there is so much more to be discovered.

Looking at the clock, and thinking of the energy released from the apple, I wonder if I begin to understand a little of the way the Holy Spirit works in our lives. So much potential lies hidden, unused, in each of us, put there by God. We're unaware of it, but when his finger touches us and we open in response, energies are released which can transform us. Potential changes to reality, giving us the power to do his will. Sometimes we turn the metaphor round and say we need to plug into God's power. I suggest the power's already there within us, put there by him, waiting for the release commitment brings. After all, we are made in his image. Let's rejoice in it, and use the energies he gives us.

Lord, the clock's in front of me,
pulsing the seconds,
adding the minutes.
Reminding me not only of the time
but of your power.

The wonder of it.
The universe modelled in deep intricacies,
lovingly interlocked.
Each form, each process
fashioned with creator-care.
In the vast sweep of your purposes
nothing forgotten,
each tiny section jewelled in joy.
Energy that fuels the sun
secreted softly in the smallest part.
Waiting for release.
Available and free.

Lord, touch my life
with that same hand
that fingered all to being.
Unlock the bars that hold me back,
and draw me out
into the mainstream of your purposes.

Turn latent energies to use.
Give me a new dynamic
that I may reach, in you,
all that I can be.
Live out the possibilities
that in your love
you've planted in my life.

# Luke 15:11-24

IN his book *The Way of the Heart,* Henri Nouwen calls our sinful nature a "false self", built up by the pressures of the world we live in. He suggests that only in an encounter with the loving God do we find our real selves. He calls this a furnace of transformation. In it, all our defences are burnt away until we face our individual nothingness, and throw ourselves on his mercy. Then the wounds are healed by the love revealed to us, and we start becoming our real selves.

The book is a challenging study of the spirituality of the Desert Fathers (there were some Mothers too!), early Christian mystics who developed solitary lives of contemplation and meditation in the first few centuries after Christ. Nouwen writes with an insight and an apparent simplicity, which goes very deep.

The "false self" idea strikes a chord of recognition with me. Many folk look on themselves, and on others, as though we were all by nature sinful. We assume that to be the norm, and we understand, or mis-understand, our encounter with Jesus Christ as an experience that transforms us into something "super" human, which somehow puts us on a higher plane of living. Paul, it's true, says that in Christ we are new creatures, but that I believe is in the sense of transformation from one state to another, and without implying that we become in any way superhuman. Surely, in Christ we become, not superhuman, but truly human. God created us for fellowship with him, and it follows that our original nature was capable of that. But since the rot set in, we grow up handicapped by the world and our acceptance of it, and it's only an encounter with God which re-forms us into what we were meant to be. Truly human.

The same thing is implied in the story of the Prodigal Son. When he realises how far he's fallen he "comes to his senses" or "comes to himself", depending on your translation of Luke 15. Again, the conclusion I draw is that in his disorientated, alienated life he is not himself. He is living this false self, and only in reunion with his father and his family, can he fully celebrate his humanity. It's the same with us. Only in this reunion with God and the family of God can we be what we are meant to be, real men and women.

"True encounter with Christ liberates something within us, a power we did not know we had, a capacity to grow and change," as Thomas Mertin said.

Lord, faced with my daily failures,
it's so easy to despair.
To think that all I see is all there is,
and that the one I seem to be,
weak and hurting, is the real me.
To think that all I can expect,
along the way I walk,
is more of the same.
A bit bleak, Lord, a bit daunting.

But then I hear your voice,
telling the criticising crowd
the story of the son come home.
It makes me realise that I, like him,
am made for better things.
That wallowing among the pigs and dirt,
the shoe-shine brightness of my promises smeared over,
is not where I should be.

Remind me, Lord, when I look down to that,
that I'm created in your image.
That I was meant, am meant,
to live and walk with you.
That in your purposes and love,
I can stand straight and whole.
That, living in the life
your son has bought and given me,
I can return to what I truly am.
Your child. Real and fulfilled.

Then in the joy of knowing that's for me,
I walk the world refreshed.
My feet still firmly planted on the ground,
but moving with new grace and dignity.

And Lord, remind me, in my joy restored,
that those whom I look down on —
yes, Lord, I do — are in your image too.
Help me to see through your wide eyes,
the worth of those I meet today.
Respect and honour them as your creation.
To see their true humanity

*however scuffed and muddied over,*
*and welcome them, as you have welcomed me,*
*into the family.*

COTSWOLD MEADOWS

# John 16:31-33

THE Sunday morning communion service ended with the familiar words: "Go forth into the world in peace. . . ." I've heard them many times, taking them sometimes as comfort, sometimes as a ritual ending, sometimes only half hearing because I'm already trying to remember which pocket my car keys are in. This time they came as a challenge: my role as a Christian is not simply — if it is simple — to live with Christ's peace in my heart. It is to live that peace in the world, not for my benefit, but for the world's. To do that positively in my relationships isn't to practise the doormat humility of the weak, letting others walk over me out of fear and then dressing it up as Christian meekness. It is a creative force stemming from a real understanding of Christ's purposes for humankind.

The peace I experience isn't to be protected from the harsh winds of reality by withdrawing from the world and sheltering in dreams of the coming Kingdom. It's to be used to change and temper the world of which I'm a functioning part. Too often we try to hide in a private "Christian" world, instead of working to establish God's kingdom here and now. I imagine those words as part of the job description given to Jesus, and by him to us, not as a pious hope, but for positive action. Jesus lived out that peace. He sought out the troubled, the anxious and sick, confronted the angry and vindictive, and faced them with peace. He refused to be provoked into spite or pettiness, or be diverted from its purpose.

It's a vulnerable role. Jesus the baby is at the mercy of inhospitable innkeepers and despotic rulers. Jesus the man is at the mercy of violent soldiers and the bigoted religious. The Son of God is in the hands of evil forces. Yet he triumphed in the strength of peace, and that triumph sets our lives in a perspective of hope. Not for us the hopeless, existential acceptance of whatever comes in pain and dreariness. Rather, the joyous realisation that the lines of life move to a meeting point beyond the horizon we see, and that the whole earth is moving towards that meeting. The journey may be rough and full of conflict, but through Jesus in the stable and Christ on the cross my energy, emotions and anger can be transformed into creative acts of peace within that perspective.

Peace, Lord.
They were talking about it on radio this morning.
And yesterday. And the day before.
No peace from peace!
I'm sure we all want it,
but I'm not sure we all know what we mean.
Or mean the same thing.

It's so easy to oversimplify.
Settle for the easiest.
Go home. Turn the key in the lock.
Draw the curtains, sit down and relax. Peace.
The trouble is, there's always somebody outside
knocking on the door of my conscience.
Disturbing my peace with their needs.
I try to ignore them, tell them to go next door,
someone else's problem.
But they go on knocking, and when I open up,
ready to give them a piece of my mind,
the only one standing there is you.
Calling me from the false quiet of my cocooned comfort
back into the world.

You promised me peace, Lord.
But when I look at your life,
as honestly as I can,
I realise that peace
isn't a "Reader's Digest" offer, exclusively for me,
selected out of millions.
Nothing to do but claim it
by sending back the envelope, post free.
But something to be found only in you,
and your demands.

Your seed of peace grows to fruition in reality.
The tree of life is not some pampered sapling,
glass-covered from cold wind and frost.
It's a strong oak, scarred' and battered,
the evidence of struggle in twisted branch and furrowed bark,
but deep rooted in the soil of your kingdom.
No easy way to go.
A cross-road, if you get my meaning.

*What's that? Oh yes, I see.*
*It's your meaning, your road.*
*And the only way to your peace.*

*I'll work at it, Lord.*

SUMMER SAIL, SCOTLAND

# Ephesians 2:13-19

"HILL STREET BLUES" is a fictional TV cops and robbers series which is rough and tough, but much more honest than many other similar programmes. People talk true. They're seen as human and vulnerable, reaching for the right, often failing but always hoping. A recent programme ended with the successful capture of a group of vicious young men. One detective is happy. "That's that," he says, "We've nailed them!" The other detective sees deeper. Anguished, he replies, "Yes, but where do you put the hate?"

What was he to do with the violence of his own feelings towards the criminals, or to the society that produces them? What was he to do with the anger, the hurt, that was pulling him all ways?

Isn't that a key question for any human being to ask? We hide the hate, the anger; perhaps religious people specially. We gloss over it, hoping it'll just go away. But it's still there, in me anyway. It may be covered over, but it bubbles up at the slightest provocation, from an apparently bottomless reservoir.

Where do you put it all? The answer's in Paul's words: "For (Jesus) is himself our peace . . . he has made us one, and in his own body . . . has broken down the enmity . . ." (Ephesians 2:14).

But I still have a problem. I can, and do, accept the truth of those words — that Christ took the world's hate and anger, including mine, and killed it. The trouble is, it's a long time dying. It still kicks and struggles whenever I'm hurt or frustrated.

The reality of honest Christian living can be hard to face. We so often try, and sometimes succeed in, deceiving ourselves that everything's fine, until the crunch comes. The war's won, but the battle's not over. Yet he is our peace, the source of life and strength. He's standing ready to squeeze a little more love into my life whenever I let him help me squeeze out a little more of the hate. It's a struggle, but I know he'll help me keep up the fight.

Lord, still it happens.
The love I think I hold so dear
sits light upon the lid
that closes off the violence inside.
With each new provocation,
real or imaginary,
it bubbles up,
explodes the cover of my self control.
My life a killing ground
where anger rules.
Walks unconcerned over the bones of good intentions,
half buried in resentment's mud.

The tension stretches taut to breaking point
until I look to you.
No hope within myself.
You are my peace . . .
The affirmation that I make,
I make in faith
that slowly it may reach reality.
I'm not there yet.
You've won the war,
but each small skirmish,
still has the feel of battle.

Give me the courage, Lord,
to follow through the war within myself
until the enmity is gone.
Until I stand in peace,
the flak jacket of conflict thrown away,
and clothed in love.

# Matthew 5:38-43

I READ of a scientist who'd studied bees for years. He'd weighed and measured and analysed. Finally, he decided that with the bee's shape and weight, and the form of its wings, it was impossible for it to fly. It broke all the rules.

Fortunately, no one told the bees. So millions of them continue to buzz around the world, doing the impossible every day.

Doing the impossible is a Christian commitment. Loving your neighbour is possible, depending on your neighbour, but loving your enemy? Not retaliating to insult is just possible, but turning the other cheek? Can you really give your coat to the man who's already taken your shirt? It's just too much to ask. Yet Jesus sees it as everyday life for his followers.

I imagine some scientist from outer space looking at the situation. Setting human behaviour and actions against the demands the Christian faith makes, pondering deeply and deciding it can't work. Actually, we don't need to think of an outer space visitor, there are plenty of people near at hand who tell us that the Christian life doesn't work, and can't work.

But if we look around honestly, we can pick out individuals whose lives prove it does. People who've overcome the instinctive defence, the selfish response, and who live something better. You can't easily define it, but you can feel it. You can't weigh it, but you know it's there. Experience tells you. Life contains values we can't measure, and which modify the "facts" in ways we can't always understand.

It's one result of God living in us. God in human life? Another impossible, but true. A God of resurrection, something that doesn't happen, but did. And if that can happen then a real change in our life style is both believable and possible. Paul writes, "I have strength for anything through him who gives me power" (Philippians 4:13). He was writing from personal experience, not theory, and we can call on the same strength.

To be fair to the scientist, there was some humour in his report. He knew bees could fly — he'd watched them for years. His point was that it went against the rules, which showed that what we know isn't everything. Leave room in your life for the impossible.

Doing the impossible, Lord,
is just a bit daunting.
I'm only human,
with all the weaknesses and hesitations
that implies.
I've got my dreams,
the things I want to do,
and that includes my life with you.
I try to set my standards near to yours.
Take on the attitude that puts you first,
the set of mind that opens up my life
to living as you lived.
But what I'm conscious of, much of the time,
is living down from my ideals,
not living up to yours.

It really takes a quantum leap to follow you.
Flying would be easy.
And yet you ask it.
That has to mean it's not impossible at all.
Love couldn't ask impossibilities
and let me buzz around,
frantic, in an endless maze of effort,
going nowhere.
I see it's difficult,
and those who say it's easy
I think don't look too closely at themselves.
It's difficult, but possible.
You proved that
through your life in Jesus.
Through other people too.
"I can do all things . . ."
That's quite a claim, but Paul was just a man.
Human, like me.
And if he found it true,
could find the strength to live,
and work, and face the world, creatively.
then so can I.

Lord, when I feel the doubts
creep up on me again,
anchoring me heavily to earth

*lead weighted, heavy footed,*
*just send a bee.*
*And in its flight I'll see your power,*
*and all the possibilities in me.*

SILVER BIRCHES

# 2 Timothy 1:11-14

A PRIEST was being interviewed on radio. He'd been working in a part of Africa where people's lives had been devastated by an earthquake, and the release of poison gas which had killed many. The questioner asked, "What did you say to the survivors?"

What do you say to people whose lives have been rocked by sudden tragedy? My reaction was that it's a time to listen and help, not to make statements. First, because I have no easy answer to that sort of event. And second, because I don't think people can take in much of what you say, anyway, when their minds are brimming with anxiety and fear. People in shock are not searching for explanations, they are crying out for comfort. That goes beyond reasoned argument, back to a basic need to feel they're not alone. They want to know that someone cares. They need to feel arms round them, something, someone, to ease the pain.

God's love becomes real in these situations, not through sermons, but through quiet listening. They need our time, and maybe our tears, but not our logic.

One thing helps me. When Paul wrote to Timothy, with all his experience of pain and persecution, he affirmed, "I know *whom* I have believed". Paul believed in a person, not a philosophy. It wasn't ideas or words, but a presence who gave him the courage to go on. Faced with desperate people, isn't our job to crystallise his love and presence through ours? Not in sermons, but in the warmth of practical caring. The explanation can come later, when people realise they are loved.

Words, Lord, again.
Dripping like water from a leaking tap.
Wetting my feet,
launching my ego on a sea of platitudes.
Their only purpose to fill the spaces
between my questions.
Padding the sharp corners of my uncertainties.
Spoken only because I find
that listening's harder.

Lord, if I'm faced with someone's need today,
help me to offer silence.
Not in the coldness of indifference,
but in warm welcome
to hear his version of events.
Help me control the urge to talk,
to people his life with my puppets,
to jump to safe conclusions,
for which I have stock answers.

Teach me, with open mind and heart,
to hear his words and thoughts.
To substitute the clichés I mistake for truth
with quiet love.
Spoken through eyes, not mouth,
in hand, not sermon.
In love, that comes before advice.

I see your hand reach out to touch
before you spoke the words.
And in the fellowship of shared perplexity,
the still moment,
I know there will be three of us,
not two.
An Emmaus road,
on which you walk with us,
dispelling doubt.
making the moment vibrant,
eloquent,
not with words,
but with your presence.

# Luke 15:25-32

I 'VE been reading the story of the Prodigal Son yet again. It's so full of insight into human character, and deep understanding of the way people behave. On this reading, it was the elder brother who got my sympathy. Just read the story in Luke 15, and concentrate on verses 25-32.

There's the elder brother, out on the farm. On his way back home he hears the celebrations and, when he learns it's for his wild brother's return, he gets angry. I have the feeling that I would have done too. He was taken so much for granted; treated with no more consideration than the farm machinery. No one even bothered to send a message to him to say his brother was back. No warning about the welcome-home party. He had to ask a servant.

"I've worked hard for you," he reproaches his father, "I've always been available, never been a nuisance, always helped, but when have you acknowledged it?" "Son," says the father, trying to paper over the cracks, "You're always with me, everything I have is yours." That's just the point. Because he was always there, the elder son was taken for granted. If "everything I have is yours" it would have been helpful if he'd been consulted, and asked to help with the party; and asked for his agreement to liquidate more assets — if that's how you describe the fatted calf!

These little human details give me a warning about taking people for granted. If you appreciate someone, make sure they know. If you value the work they do, tell them. If someone is always available, always willing to share in what goes on, acknowledge it. It's far better to do it *now*, than try to comfort hurt feelings later. Love should never be assumed, people need to know and feel it.

Don't misunderstand. I'm not trying to devalue the story. I know its main point is about the breadth of God's forgiveness, and forgiveness is far more important than anything else. It was something the elder son would have to face up to in forgiving both his brother and his father, but it might have come easier if he'd been drawn earlier into the circle of appreciative love.

Lord, I know just how he felt,
the elder brother. No one told him.
No one thought of him, except in passing.
He didn't seem to matter very much.
And when he heard
all that was being done
for one who'd had his chance, and blown it,
I understand the slow hurt creeping in.
The joy he might have felt at his brother's return
overlaid by an invisible dust of destructiveness.
And from the dust a cancer of resentment grew,
springing from the fallout of his anger,
poisoning relationships.

I, too, can feel this hurt,
this irritation that rubs sore
the vulnerable heel of my pride.
But when I do, Lord,
give me the sensitivity to realise
that others feel the same.
That as I step back in protest and dismay
I may not tread on their vulnerability.

Then, give me too, Lord,
arising from my pain, power to forgive.
Simply, not selfrighteously.
So easy, sometimes, to bestow forgiveness
as a rich gift to undeserving poor,
when all the time the one who needs forgiveness most
is me.

Help me to feel their hurt as well as mine.
And then, in deeper understanding still,
to see the pain is yours.
Yours the vulnerability
stretched on the cross of my indifference.
Yours the forgiveness
covering not just my small hurts,
but all the world's.
And, Lord, in mercy and in love
let me experience not just forgiveness
but forgiving.

# Job 38:1-12

ON holiday in Scotland, we had a cottage on the shore of Loch Awe. It's a long lake, if Scots will forgive me calling a loch a lake! One arm of the loch runs to the sea through a narrow, winding, rocky river bed. It's a great place for salmon, and there are several "leaps", places where deep pools and shallow water are separated by tumbling waterfalls. It's exciting to watch these places. The mature salmon return instinctively from the sea to the river where they were born, and swim upstream to breed. The shallows and the falls block their way. Suddenly, the water flurries into foam. A great salmon, 10 or 12 pounds or more, leaps in a bright flash of silver, over the fall into clear deep water beyond. Sometimes the fish makes it first jump. Sometimes it falls back, quietly to regain its energy and explode again into urgent action.

Another day I watched an old craftsman remaking a dry-stone wall. It's a centuries-old skill. The wall is made without mortar of any kind. Rough stones are fitted together with care enough for the wall to stand for a hundred years and more. He worked slowly, choosing each stone with great patience. Long, flat stones as strengthening bonds; heavy, chunky stones to anchor them; smaller, rounder stones to fill the spaces in an intricate jigsaw puzzle; little wedge stones to lock in the larger, and bring stability to the whole.

What a contrast. The salmon, all flashing energy and speed. The craftsman with quiet judgement, infinite patience. Two ways of working. We can't say one is right, the other wrong. We can only recognise the value of different approaches for different purposes, the variety of temperament, and pray for wisdom to use the appropriate one for each situation. God's purposes are fulfilled in both. He created the salmon and the craftsman, and I believe he rejoices in both: ". . . and God saw all that he had made, and it was very good" (Genesis 1:31).

You created both, Lord.
Salmon and stonemason.
You command the urgent leap,
the quick silver flash of shining scale,
the taut whiplash of muscle,
curving high over foam furrows.
Moving upstream to the urgency, the ecstasy, ahead.

Yours, too, the slow coordination of work-hardened hands.
The deliberate judgement of country wisdom
weighing stone against stone.
Searching the edge, the shape, the space-filling form.
The quiet, reflective building of the wall,
each stone a cornerstone, essential to the whole.

Creation shouts with joy
at the endless change of pattern
in the kaleidoscope of your will.
Sometimes, Lord, I gasp
at the sudden, shining revelation of your purpose.
You move ahead of me, dancing shimmering in light.
My muscles knot, my breath gives out in the effort to follow.
And then you throw me, Lord.
The pace changes.
Movement so slow I fail to notice it.
I grow impatient at snail speed,
looking for one small indication of what I am to do,
and where to go.

Bewildering, Lord.
I look for logic, search for balance,
anxious for easy understanding.
And then your voice comes, gently, sometimes sternly —
the same variety of pattern —
asking where was I when you laid the earth's foundations?

I know, Lord. Your world, not mine.
And though through weight and measure
we predict the movements of creation,
we can't predict the mind of the creator.
For me, just the assurance that it's yours.
And that you care.

# Isaiah 55:6-11

WHAT shape is God? Donald English, a notable Christian preacher, was speaking about John Baptist in prison. John sends messengers to Jesus. "Are you the one who is to come?" they ask, on John's behalf.

We can only try to imagine, and that not very well, what was going on in John's mind. According to Donald English, the basic issue was really about the shape of God. John had his own mental picture of the Messiah and apparently Jesus didn't quite fit the pattern. He didn't quite act the way John expected him to. Donald English hears Jesus throwing the question back, "John, am I to be your shape, or are you going to be my shape?"

To some degree we all create God in our own image. Hopefully, we've left behind the nice-old-gentleman-with-a-white-beard, but we each hold a picture in our minds. Perhaps of a merciful God, or a judgmental one; a father, a brother, or a lover. Some suggest we should think of God as mother. Whatever the picture, we tend unconsciously to select and arrange our experiences of life to confirm the image we already hold. We neatly file away and forget the signs that tell us the disturbing news that God is bigger than our ideas. Yet he is not to be confined in the little box of my prejudices, or the straitjacket of my timidity.

Maybe it would be more comfortable if he were. Holding on to God is sometimes a bit like holding an elephant by the tail — you have to go in his direction, not yours. And his direction leads to expanding horizons: "... for as the heavens are higher than the earth, so are my ways higher than your ways and my thoughts than your thoughts" (Isaiah 55:9).

It is God who holds us in the palm of his hand, not the other way round. He encourages and stimulates us to explore, to learn more, to move on to new riches. And in doing so we slowly assume *his* shape, modelled into his likeness.

Lord, I reach out my hand
blindly fingering your features.
Stretch out my mind
to encompass your infinity.
Open my whole being
to absorb the universe that you created.
And I can't.

". . . for as the heavens are higher than the earth. . . ."

Lord, I acknowledge in unusual humility
— it doesn't fit me very well,
it's like a Sunday suit brought out
and pressed for wear occasionally,
but mostly stored away, unused —
that I can't hope to understand or analyse
the working of your mind,
or fit you to the pattern of my life.
Too high, too wide, too deep.

And yet my ego struggles,
tries again to make and remake you
in my own image,
reduce you to the smallness of my thought.
I raise the golden idol of my plans,
bow down and worship,
and hope that you will sanctify the act.
But when I do I feel the sudden quiet,
the loneliness, of your absence.
Not that you've gone away
but that, in pushing you away, I've moved myself.
And as you, lovingly, reach out across the distance of my will
and draw me back,
break down the walls of my small understanding,
unlock the doors, unbar the gates,
unlatch the windows of my mind
to the fresh wind of all that you would teach,
Lord, hold me near.

And in these moments of surprise
when, open eyed, I see your majesty;
when, open mouthed, I flounder

in the sea of your infinity,
reach out your hand to me.
Teach me to swim within the current of your love.
And in the frightening realisation of my own smallness
Show me the greatness of your care.

SUMMER FIELDS, COTSWOLDS

# Psalm 139:1-12

WHEN my last book of prayers was published, I wondered how to describe it. It weighs 154 grams. It is 21 by 15 centimetres, and has 90 pages. The paper is white, made from a precise recipe of wood cellulose, china clay, and other ingredients. The pages are covered in black ink (formula available), which forms patterns of repeated shapes, called an alphabet, plus a few dots and dashes. I could then describe the cover picture, the binding processes, and so on.

Yet when I'd said everything, I'd have said nothing. Nothing of the book's meaning. Nothing of the thought, writing, correcting. Nothing of the work of other people in producing it. Nothing of the aims and hopes in sharing thoughts, in trying to communicate with others.

Some folk analyse the world like that. They study the processes of geology and geography; the "laws" of chemistry and physics; ecology and environment. They weigh, measure and describe. And when they've done, they've said little about its real meaning and purpose. Nothing about the love and pain, the joy and sorrow of life. Nothing about the creator, or the power that sustains it. The psalmist had less facts, but a greater grasp of the essentials: "Such knowledge is beyond my understanding, so high I cannot reach it" (Psalm 139:6). And without that knowledge, the equation is incomplete. The psalmist pauses there and says, "I will praise thee, for thou dost fill me with awe. . . ."

Many of today's people, arrogant in partial learning, claim that what can't be measured or described doesn't exist. Carlo Carretto writes, "God is simple and we make him complicated. He is close to us and we make him far away. . . . The true secret of making contact with God is littleness, simplicity of heart, poverty of spirit: all the things that pride, wealth, and cleverness foil in us." (From his book *I Sought and I Found.*) We analyse when we should accept, dissect when we should worship, try to make God our shape and in the process diminish, not him, but ourselves. If love could be measured, there'd be a limit to it. Thank God for love's infinity.

Lord, in the smallness of the world I draw around me,
comforting, like a baby's blanket,
I'm at the centre.
I analyse and measure, weigh, describe,
break down the world, your world, into compartments.
Pigeonhole its processes and laws.
Take comfort in the few cold facts that I can comprehend
and, in the coldness, freeze out the love.

I take the knife of logic
and dissect the body of your creation.
Pick over, like a bright-eyed crow,
the bare bones of knowledge.
The soft murmur of your voice smothered in statistics.
And in the end all I possess
is a bad case of numbers.

Lord, it's all too big for me,
your world, your plans, your love.
It leaves me floundering in immensity.
Help me to drop the measuring tools of my arrogance.
Forgive my feeling that I have a right to know,
and that I could,
given an A-level in Divine Creativity,
begin to understand.
Even advise you, on minor things of course.
I know my limits!
Help me to raise my eyes
above the level of particularities
and, awed yet unafraid,
accept your presence here and now.

Teach me to praise you.
Let me see, in this vast universe around me,
your strength and power.
Help me to hear
in the deep reverberations of your creation,
the voice of love and tenderness.
I can't begin to understand,
can never grasp the intricate perfection of your will.
But I can touch, and feel the warmth.
Lord, let that be enough.

# Psalm 8

I WAS watching an athlete on a high wire. A straight and narrow path, if ever there was one! The skill seems to lie in confidence and balance. As the athlete walks the wire, he corrects the everpresent tendency to overbalance by gently shifting his centre of gravity towards the other side. It's a continual compensation, a living with tension, without overbalancing in any direction. It also needs a sensitive feel for the wire underfoot.

As Christians we need a similar balance, and it's hard to find. We often overemphasise one side of the truth as though it were the whole thing, and the result is a wobble that almost makes us fall off the wire. Looking at the glory and immensity of God's universe, the psalmist asks in wonder, "What is man that thou shouldst remember him?" (Psalm 8:4). We take the thought and repeat it to reaffirm our insignificance. Oh! we're ever so humble — and so we should be, because we've got it wrong. The psalmist doesn't stop there, his inspiration carries him on. "We may seem small," he says, "but God does care for us. He's made us only a little less than himself."

The miracle of human life is not that God created us at all, but that he made us great. "Little less than a god...." And when we're in danger of falling over into a faceless humility, we need the correcting balance of remembering we're made in his image. Not doormats, but children of God, with talents and abilities he can use and develop.

Sometimes of course, and some more than others, we need the correcting balance the other way. Today's world suffers from people who behave as though they were gods, with no mystery, no responsibility, beyond them. Then we do need to look at creation's complexity and feel our smallness.

The art lies in the balance. Most high wire walkers don't just use their arms; they use a long pole, for greater stability. We can do a certain amount on our own, waving our arms about, but for real balance we need the help that holding on to Jesus gives. It takes practice, particularly to lose the self-consciousness; but the time comes when balance seems natural, we can forget it, and get on with walking across the wire.

Lord, there are moments
when I just can't get my balance.
When I'm pulled one way, then another.
So many pressures and demands.
Times when I'm scared to move.
When the effort of putting one foot in front of the other
is a major problem that needs a deep breath,
and all the courage I can find.
There's a great emptiness all round me,
and whichever way I look, it's down.

I freeze. At least, I would
if my arms weren't waving frantically,
using all my energy just standing there.
It must look funny from the outside,
but to me, it hurts!
The classic clown, all red nose and tears.

I curl myself small,
nose to tail, hedgehog-hesitant,
a vulnerable bundle waiting to be flattened
by the heavy wheels of my own fears.
And yet I cling to that one truth
that you have made me
only a little lower than a god.

Made in your image.
The glory for the taking.
The glory, not only of creation,
but of creator.
Too big to take in all at once,
but something I can learn to live with.
And in the confidence,
born out of cowardice that throws me on to you,
I can step out, slowly at first,
then quicker,
knowing that your safety net of love
spreads out beneath me,
catching me when I fall,
bouncing me back to where I belong.
With you.

# John 12:20-26

ELECTION campaigns are fought mainly on television these days, and at times it's hard to tell whether a programme is a political speech or an advertisement for a new brand of analgesic — something to take the pain away. The overwhelming emphasis is on ourselves. The major political parties produce manifestos which are, as I'm sure they are in most countries, materialistic and selfish. How much this party will reduce income tax, and how much more money will appear in the wage packet. Each group seducing us into expecting more than we have a right to, and persuading us that happiness is coin-shaped.

I was wondering about the effects of a political manifesto that began: "Except a grain of wheat fall into the ground and die...." It would raise many eyebrows, but few votes, yet it's a lesson we all have to learn. We expect too much for ourselves, and from other people. Flanney O'Connor, an American woman writer, died recently at the age of 39. After years of chronic illness she wrote: "To expect too much is to have a sentimental view of life, and this is a softness that ends in bitterness". And to "sentimental", I suggest we add "and greedy".

It is the superficial, unthinking expectations we have of other people which are so easily disappointed and which can lead us to despair. Expectations we often have no right to hold. We expect our colleagues, senior or junior, to contribute to our plans and assumptions, to our wellbeing. We define the terms, set the standards, and judge the results (all without bias, of course!), and when we are disappointed we say, "Oh, he's just impossible to work with...."

But to despair of people is an injustice to God, to paraphrase Michel Quoist. Perhaps the reason a colleague doesn't live up to our expectations, apart from whether the assumptions were right or not, is that we haven't given the right help, or never listened to his ideas. Maybe the emphasis in my personal life, as in political life, needs to change from "What do I expect?" to "What can I give?" I detect an unconscious arrogance at times in some Christians who, because they have "given themselves in service" feel they then have a right to make demands on others. But giving, once begun, has to go on and, although it can be tough, it is the only valid way of life I know.

I see the growing wheat Lord.
Green and lush.
The soft summer wind stroking its hand
over the curves of the field, gentle, caressing.
Moving to a golden fulfilment.
An air of contentment, languid, warm.

I need to jog myself awake!

The old trap, reset and sprung again.
I'm happy with the images of plenty,
providing me with what I need, and want.
Not always the same thing.

Conveniently, I forget that life springs
new-nurtured out of sacrifice.
That grain must fall, lose light,
die in the darkness,
and that wheat roots tangle underground
with the dead husk of seed.

Less comfortable, Lord, that picture.
But truer.
The rough-stoned reality of your voice
so easily overlaid
with the soft rendering of the admen,
vinyl silk smooth,
this world's prophets at ten percent.

Lord, help me to see,
with the clear clarity of Christ's vision,
that life is more than these.
That in the economics of eternity
all gain is loss, loss gain.
Accountancy reborn in love.

And love, self-giving, free,
so difficult,
counts everything
by counting nothing.

# 1 Peter 1:1-7

LIFE in cities seems far removed from the farm. Harvest festivals seem unreal, remnants of former days. Many see the first fruits of harvest as an opportunity for higher prices and bigger profits rather than as an offering to God. Yet we still depend on the soil, and at harvest we remember again the cycle of death and life, of hope springing from the dying seed.

The farmer sows in hope. It's an active hope, because he also works to secure it. He tills the soil, feeds and irrigates it. This is Christian hope too. Peter tells us that we are given ". . . new birth into a living hope by the resurrection of Jesus Christ . . ." (1 Peter 1:3).

Living hope, active, developing, growing. Not a passive acceptance that everything will be all right in the end, but a hope in which we work with God to achieve his purposes. Again, it's hope which springs from the dying seed. It comes from the death of Jesus, and from the deaths that we die in actively living for him. No one comes to personal faith except by dying. The revelation of our human condition, as we see ourselves in his light, is the death of pride and self-delusion. We face the reality, and the living Christ smashes "the fetters of our intellect and lets our desperation out of hiding", as Calvin Miller puts it.

We are desperate and full of fear. The trouble is that fear is living too. It feeds on itself and creates the very things it's afraid of. It's only by facing the fact of our fear and failure that we can take hold of the hope that's offered to us.

Someone suggested to me the other day that we shouldn't examine our failures. "It's too discouraging," he said. But isn't failure part of the truth we have to face? How else do we learn? The great thing is that in facing the truth about ourselves we're thrown onto Jesus as the one source of strength and life. "And so the sombre journey to the discovery of our distress is transformed into a bright journey to the discovery of grace," as Paul Tournier writes in *The Strong and the Weak*.

And that is why our hope is real and alive — because it springs direct from the living God through whom the hope of harvest and harvest of hope are fulfilled.

Lord, I live in hope.
A lovely word.
Not the cheap cliché that shrugs its shoulders,
smiles, and says it'll be all right on the night.
But a deep root that holds me firm
in the bedrock of your love.
Whatever comes.


That's what I look for, Lord.
That's how I want to live.
The trouble is,
it doesn't come to life without a struggle.
To find the hope to live by,
first I have to die.
Face the slow, painful death of self,
the transfer of power.
A freedom fight in which I die to live,
surrender to find freedom.
All topsy-turvy.


And in the death of self,
hope comes delicately,
shimmering gossamer wings
alive with light.
Lifting the old drabness of despair
with rainbow glow.
Painting my life with new reality.


I hope for hope, Lord.
The seeds of light
sown in the darkness round your cross,
germinate, and flower and fruit
in the fallow fields of my small life.
My hope starts in your death and resurrection.
Continues in the certainty of your presence.
Fulfils itself in the clear calm confidence
of final victory.


For now, I cling to hope's small seedling.

*Vulnerable. Not yet full grown.*
*Measuring each day*
*in the new leaves of little victories*
*and, help me, Lord, often in small defeats.*
*But still I cling to hope.*
*And know you walk with me.*

*Thank you, Lord.*

BEECH TREES, LAKE DISTRICT

# Romans 8:18-21

R ELAXING after a recent tour overseas, I was listening to music. First, a recording of Mahalia Jackson, the black American gospel singer, earthy, raw and emotional. Then the Royal Choral Society singing Handel's *Messiah*, two hundred voices in a glorious orchestration of sound and scripture. So different, and yet all part of the joy of life that springs from the resurrection. "The resurrection," wrote D. H. Lawrence, "is to life, not to death. Can I not then walk this earth in gladness being risen from sorrow? Is the flesh that was crucified become as poison to the crowds in the street, or is it a strong blossoming out of earth's humus?"

Yes, it still offends some, but the reality of the resurrection is a tough, enduring growth rising from the fertile soil of sacrifice. It's the ground of faith in which all our being is rooted, and from which hope and action flowers and fruits. And it's a resurrection to joy. How can I be sad and discouraged when Christ has died, and risen, for me? Passing briefly through Los Angeles I was surprised to see that Easter is treated as a family festival in the USA, rather like Christmas elsewhere, with reunions and parties. How fitting to make Easter a time when people meet together in love, because while Christmas tells us of God's birth into the human family, Easter gives us the new birth of human beings as part of God's family. And the joy of it lies in our unity in him, who is the origin, and source of power, the focus of all creation. In his *Hymn of the Universe* Teilhard de Chardin wrote:

> "Lord . . .
> when it was given me to see
> where the dazzling trail
> of particular beauties
> and partial harmonies was leading,
> I recognized that it was all
> coming to centre on a single point
> A single person:
> yourself . . .
>
> Thus all lines converge,
> complete one another. Interlock.
> All things are now but one.

It is the vision of Paul, seeing all creation waiting "with eager expectation for God to reveal his sons . . . and to enter the liberty and splendour of the children of God" (Romans 8:19).

Not some distant dream, Lord,
a mirage dancing insubstantial in shimmering air,
but reality.
Your resurrection.
Leaving the grave empty and impotent.
Doubts discarded,
down in a corner with the grave clothes.
Convincing by its new life.

Urgent in energy.
Not edging gently round the heavy stone
but pushing through. Vibrant.
Its roots growing, thickening,
taking hold of the small particles of my life,
compacting the shifting sand into firm ground,
strong enough to stand on.
Strong enough to face the pounding waves.
Growing new leaves of hope and joy,
their shade refreshing, invigorating.

And in this miracle of life is born another.
This plant of life itself becomes the soil
in which I grow.

My own roots grow strong
in the rich soil of your life.
I leaf, blossom, fruit in you.
Find reassurance
in the defeat of death.
Still to be faced, when time comes,
but faced with the joy
of knowing the stone is rolled away.
Already.

Hallelujah.

# 1 Corinthians 13:8-13

A PHRASE sticks in my mind from recent reading. . . . "Truth on its way to being truer. . . ." Can something true become truer? In absolute terms, no, it's either true or it isn't. But, in terms of our understanding of truth, surely the answer is yes. Our understanding is only partial, and our grasp of the truth something that has to develop and mature. An apple's an apple from the first swelling of the bud, but there's little joy trying to eat it at that stage. It needs time to ripen.

If we could grasp that it would save so much pain and conflict. We fight so hard to protect "the truth", yet often we are only fighting to protect our own imperfect understanding of it. Like children, we cling to our first experiences. We hold tight to a few proof texts we learnt in our spiritual adolescence, as though that was the limit of what God has to teach us. Really, the truth we know is only the hors-d'oeuvre, a first course to whet our appetite for what comes later. The problem is that we're too insecure to follow the truth wherever it leads; we prefer to cage it, tame it, pretend that we possess it all.

Truth has to move on, not abandoning but enriching what went before. The end result is a deeper truth that may look very different from our original version. I remember an early orchestral concert in my teens. The power and drive of Sibelius' Second Symphony floored me. It opened my mind to new things, but it's not the only music I listen to now.

Truth is a life-long, inner pursuit, but we make it with him: we in him, he in us (John 17:21,23). The truth lives in us, encouraging, leading us into deeper truth; and helping us to work it out in daily living.

"God is on the point of your pencil, on the edge of your ploughshare," as Teilhard de Chardin says. I'm not sure I grasp the full meaning of that, but it contains the assurance that he's part of my life, sharing what I do, what I am. Even sharing my search for deeper truth, and leading me into it.

It's comforting, Lord, to think I have the truth,
the whole truth, and nothing but the truth.
Reassuring, to peg the world down,
hold it fast in the chains of my small knowledge.
Tie it up and relax.

But Lord, the truth's a sleeping giant.
And when he wakes
all my Lilliputian certainties are torn out, screaming,
by a twitch of his hand.
My little dogmatisms damaged past repair.

Your truth stands towering over me.
However far I reach on tiptoe,
however much I try,
it stays beyond my reach.
Too great to hold, too high to comprehend.

Forgive my arrogance.
I can't reach further than truth's shoelace
and yet I claim to know it all.
I try to tame you,
hold you in the cage of my timidity.
Make you predictable and safe.
The truth is —
and there I go again, Lord, telling you —
it frightens me to think that all the world I see out there
is only a beginning.
That as I walk, hesitating, towards the far horizon
it moves away.
However much I see and learn, there's more.
And what I hold, though precious, is still partial,
the dim image of the glories yet to come.

Lord, turn my mind around.
Help me to realise that what I see
as never-ending quest, a constant learning,
is not a threat, but an adventure, lived with you.
Help me to understand that the infinity that beckons me,
is an infinity of love.

And as I take the road afresh, each day,

*I'm not sure where it leads, or where I'm going,*
*but I'm going there with you.*
*And that's enough.*

COUNTRY BRIDGE, CUMBRIA

# Romans 14:7-13

WHATEVER the problem, someone can always oversimplify it. Sometimes a problem *is* simpler than it seems at first sight, and a cool mind can point to an easy answer. More often though, the simple answers don't really meet the case. A great scientist of an earlier day, Sir Arthur Eddington, once said that we often think that when we have completed our study of one, we know all about two, because "two is one and one". We forget that we still have to make a study of "and".

There's an important point here, an extra factor in the equation. Whether we are dealing with fellow humans, or even with observed "scientific fact", one and one often makes more than two, because there's a relationship as well as a number. There's a mysterious chemistry that alters things, just through their being together. One thing which makes painting so fascinating and demanding is allowing for this. Put a spot of bright yellow paint on a background of grey, and the yellow spot looks large and bright. Put an identical yellow spot on a bright blue background, and the yellow looks duller and smaller. The same colour is changed by what's around it. It's changed by relationship.

For paint, read people. Two people living and working together are not just $1 + 1 = 2$. In a good relationship, they become more than simple addition. G. K. Chesterton said enthusiastically that to have an ally made you, not two, but two thousand. A bad relationship discounts them and the two may even become a minus quantity through the unhappiness and personal diminishment it creates.

The progression to Christian living is an obvious one. There's an extra factor, which isn't extra at all. A factor which adds or subtracts from the living equation of our relationships, leaving them richer or poorer. "For no one of us lives to himself alone," Paul tells the Christians at Rome (Romans 14:7). We live in relationship not only with each other but with the Lord, and his love is the "extra" factor. In 1 Corinthians 13, Paul reminds us that we may be able to communicate, analyse and plan, believe in all we're doing, be outgoing and outgiving, but if the "extra" factor isn't there, linking the one and the one, then it all comes to nothing.

We need to make sure that the "and" between one and one is the "and" of God; and if you want to turn it into the obvious pun then all right — it's the hand of God, in action.

Lord, there are moments, long moments,
when it seems attractive,
living to myself, alone.
Days when people make demands on me,
my time, my energy, emotions.
Times when everyone else is wrong,
and I long to disappear into my dark shell,
a hermit crab, only my claws showing.
Ready to snap at first contact.

Yet if I did, how poor I'd be.
Because rejecting their demands, I reject them.
Leave gaps in my life.
And only when the gaps are narrowed
can the spark of love flash, dance across,
warming my life with light and energy.

Lord, make me sensitive to other people's needs.
Happier to build bridges, sustain relationships.
Help me acknowledge that we're not machines,
or lumps of meat created by the accidental chemistry
of some primeval pressure cooker.
But people who need people,
and the loving kindnesses that make life good.

Then, Lord, I realise:
the very fact that I'm here now, talking to you,
gives proof of that.
I need you, need your strength and understanding.
and any thought of living to myself alone is crazy.
Rejecting other people's needs, I reject my own.
If my deep needs are real, then so are their's.

Lord, make me yours today
and, in the making,
make me other people's too.
That love may grow in me
towards them, and you.

# Philippians 3:5-14

SOMETIMES, I'm tempted to sit back and say to the Lord, with the exaggerated politeness I tend to use when I'm actually very impatient, "Lord, can you please make up your mind? In your own time, of course, but can you tell me simply and clearly exactly what you want me to do?"

You see, I've been reading two books. One, *The Way of the Heart* describes the spirituality of the early Desert Fathers that came from long solitude and deep meditation. It emphasises the importance of being, not doing. For me, it underlines our present lack of time for prayer. The second is Michel Quoist's *With Open Heart*. He's an activist. "God," writes Quoist, "isn't going to ask, What did you dream? What did you think? What did you plan? What did you preach? He's going to ask What did you do?"

So it's not enough to be, you've got to do! And we all know the lack of time for that. The easiest thing may be to stop reading and thinking, and just react to circumstances. Some do. But when you go a bit deeper things start to get clearer. The desert solitude wasn't a cop-out from the world, but a recognition of the need to have something good to offer the world — real insight, a deep awareness of God's loving nature — experiences which are found in the quiet, with God. Quoist starts at the other end of the same line and reminds me that personal Christian experience has to be turned into action. You can't keep love under glass like a specimen butterfly impaled on a pin of piety.

There's a balance needed but, being a balance, it's delicate, and we tend to overweight things one way or the other depending on temperament. Some of us rush around doing, some are quietly being, and we all wish the others were different! It's interesting to read Philippians 3. Paul tells us who he *was* — a Hebrew, a Pharisee; and what he'd *done* — zealous in work for his faith, obedient to the Law. In his new life being and doing are combined again. All he cares for is to know Christ — being — but then to press on towards the goal, putting what he knows into practice — doing (Phil. 3:14). We try for the same balance, aware, I hope, of our own bias to one side or the other, and understanding the bias of others.

Lord, the trouble is
I want it all cut and dried.
A clear path set out for me,
an easy set of instructions,
a route map I can't possibly misinterpret.
And what would I call it?
The Lazyman's Guide to the Kingdom?
And you the courier,
helping with the luggage,
moving me smoothly from one hotel to the next.
Taking care of all the problems.
Life one long holiday.

You expect more of me than that, Lord.
You show me a real world of choices,
questions I have to face, decisions to make,
tensions I must learn to balance
as I move along the road.

I need the quiet times with you.
The times when we can sort out our relationship,
just you and me.
When we can concentrate on who and what I am.
But who and what I am only become real
back in the world outside.
You were the Christ throughout your life,
but without the focus of the cross
your purpose would be blurred, half done,
and that's not done at all.

But doing needs a centre point
to give stability and strength.
A starting place, from which the purpose comes.
So one's no use without the other.
The building needs foundations.

And I begin to see my hopes for what they are.
Child's dreams of life, clear cut,
though not so innocent, and feather-cushioned from reality.
Served up, well cooked, on a warm plate.
Life's tougher than that.
The choices must be made,

*and with each choice*
*the risk of right or wrong.*
*The tensions stay, but so do you.*
*To share it with me.*

*I am content.*
*No, that's not true,*
*I'm not,*
*but I'll settle for uncertainty,*
*with you.*

WINTER'S DAY, NORFOLK.

# Luke 10:29-37

CONTRASTS: light or dark, faith or doubt, right or wrong. It's comforting to be able to classify things that way, but it's too simple. We classify so easily. Make things clear cut and precise. The problem is that life just isn't like that. In a painting, a house or a face is only "real" if light and dark complement each other, and both are needed to build up solidity and depth.

Often doubt counterpoints faith in the Christian life. After all, if there were no doubt would faith be real? Louis Evely writes "Faith is, after all, an admixture of light and darkness. We will always have enough darkness with us to justify (to ourselves) the refusal of light. But we will always have enough light to allow us to bear the darkness." And, although each one of us would like to be all light, all goodness, all faith, in fact we combine the contrasts.

Look at the story of the Good Samaritan again in Luke 10. It's a good rule not to push a parable too far beyond the point Jesus was making but think about the people in the story. Not the man who was mugged, although have you noticed how little we *do* think of him except as an object of charity? But think of the others. It's so easy to paint them all light or dark, all good or bad, and reinforce our own prejudices. I've a feeling that if we met the priest and Levite today we'd find they were "good" people. Committed church folk, sincere, loving to their families, pillars of society, paying their dues. Just too busy. A mixture of contrasts. And I guess the Samaritan would be too. Not cardboard cutouts, but human beings.

So how do we sort it out? Maybe by being a bit more honest with ourselves, and looking at our motives and assumptions a little more. I'm not suggesting a three year course in introspection, but the best way out of our prejudices is to recognise them. This won't make them go away, but it lets us begin to allow for them in our reactions. Someone said the greatest piece of unexplored territory lies between the ears. The more we know about ourselves, the more we may be able to accept the mixture of contrasts we all are. And maybe we shall then grow in understanding each other. That, I reckon, is another good way to find an answer to the question "Who is my neighbour?"

Lord, the only one I'm slow to judge
is me.
Where I'm concerned
I always see the extenuating circumstances.
And find it easy to forgive.
But turn it round,
put others in the dock,
and I bring in a verdict without hesitation.
Guilty, and with no appeal.

It's all so easy, Lord,
to find a reason to condemn.
To criticise, hold up another's faults.
Makes me feel good.
Helps me to hide the truth
of my own weaknesses
behind a mask of righteousness.
And, like a mask, empty.
Fragile as tissue, Lord,
thin as skin and yet persistent.
I see it all in black and white.
At one end or the other of the scale.

Lord, help me find the tolerance for others
that I expect from you.
The loving understanding
that gives another chance, and yet another,
like you give me.
Help me accept that every life I touch,
and touches me,
has similar confusions.
Light and dark, good and bad.
That, as I struggle with myself,
so others struggle too.
And far better that I help another up,
than pull him down.

Help me to look with eyes of love,
like yours.

## 2 Corinthians 8:7-9

I THINK it strange that when we've been gardening, something I do reluctantly, we say our hands are "dirty" or "soiled". Really they've just been in simple contact with the earth, the tangible source of life.

My travels in Asia have made me very conscious of the land. So many peasant farmers depend utterly on what it gives. To them, the land isn't "dirt". An Australian aborigine once said, "The land is our mother . . . our identity. To us land is a living thing. We are part of it and it is part of us."

Am I making it too romantic, as I sit at my polished desk? When I'm studying next year's budget I don't want even a speck of that precious earth getting between the contacts of my electronic calculator. And when I think of the exploitation of both the earth and its people there's little place for being romantic. What about the dispossessed? The many who own nothing but the soil under their finger nails?

Jesus was one of those. The pungent stable wasn't his. Even the straw belonged to others. I'm sure the gold the wise man gave him soon ran out when the refugee family moved down to Egypt. The New Testament never describes any possessions of Jesus, except the robe they stripped from him at the cross.

And yet it does. It speaks of richness, the riches of love, human contact, relationships. That richness of human experience is common to us all. I've seen the same joy in the eyes of a young mother in Nepal looking in wonder at her baby as I've seen elsewhere. The same anxiety in the face of a father as he brings his son to an Indian leprosy clinic. Humanity is one, its hopes and needs the same, and my travel emphasises our common need for the richness of Christ. It lies, not in the things we have, but in the relationships we share. In the joy of being human. In our experience of love, in our closeness to each other and to him.

Lord, it's hard to get the balance right.
When someone mentions riches,
my mind walks to the bank.
I measure it in things.
In walletfuls, in bricks and mortar.
Things you never had,
and didn't even want.
Because you knew they didn't last.

But, Lord, I'm anchored to them.
Stuck, limpet-fast, to earth,
and sometimes it seems
not all your love
can prise me loose.

And yet I know the truth.
The richness that you offer
far transcends the things I hold so tight.
And finds fulfilment,
not in holding on,
but giving up.

I know.
The trouble is
the seed of knowledge
lies quiet in my mind.
Not growing in my heart.

I need the strength
to make the move.
The jump that takes me,
joyous,
to the richness of relationship with you.

Help me to want it, Lord.
Truly.
The rest will grow from that.

# Romans 8:28-30

ONE of President Reagan's top spokesmen resigned. He said it was because he was expected to "misinform" the public at times, rather than give out the truth. There were, of course, public denials.

You can take a jaundiced view of world leaders and politicians. Those who wield power so often have "flexible" minds when it comes to the truth. Or you can rejoice at the evidence of an upright man prepared to stand against the current, and protest.

Bringing it down to an ordinary, everyday level, people do disappoint us sometimes. It's a common experience. Someone we think well of, reveals a side to his character we hadn't known or imagined. It's easy to get disillusioned.

I've been reading a book of sermons by Adrian Hastings, *In the Hurricane*. It's a challenging book. Hastings reminds us that "The incarnation . . . should render impossible too great a pessimism about man". It's easy to look at the worst in people, and expect very little. But that's not the best way. The incarnation, God becoming human in Jesus Christ, tells us very firmly that God believes in us. That he believes that we are capable of the best. It tells us that there is great potential for good in each of us, a potential that can be fulfilled through him. It reminds us that we were made for better things.

Yes, we fail, and our own and others' failure can bring us near to cynicism at times, and tempt us to expect nothing. But God goes on picking up the pieces, starts to rebuild with the scattered building blocks each time they fall down, ever patient. Christ, says Hastings, is not only proof of God's love for us, he's also proof of what God believes we can be. "For God ordained . . . that we should be shaped to the likeness of his son" (Romans 8:29). Most of us are a long way from it, but the important thing is to be facing in the right direction.

Made for better things, Lord.
Now there's a thought.
I try to believe it, but it's hard
when I look at the antics of the politicians,
the double speak, the weasel clauses
that qualify the truth and taint it.
Kill it.
Leave it where it falls, to rot.
Promises biodegradable.
Here today and none tomorrow.

It's harder still when I look inwards.
I stand knee deep in failure,
and that's on a good day.
On a bad, I'm floundering, out of my depth,
frantically sucking in the air of your forgiveness
as I go down again.

Made for better things.
Lord, I cling to it.
I hold fast to the lifeline,
thrown out in love,
that tells me that you believe in me.
It turns the world round.
Turns life and values round.
The kiss of life
that brings me back to the consciousness
of who I really am.

I've spent so much time struggling,
worrying about the weakness of my faith,
when really the truth I have to grasp is
that you believe in me.

Thank you, Lord.

# Index

# THE LEPROSY MISSION INTERNATIONAL

Headquarters: 80 Windmill Road, Brentford, Middlesex TW8 0QH, UK

| | |
|---|---|
| **Australia:** | PO Box 293, Box Hill, Victoria 3128 |
| **Belgium:** | Wolterslaan 41, 9110 St Amandsberg |
| **Canada:** | 40 Wynford Drive, Suite 216, Don Mills, Ontario M3C 1J5 |
| **Denmark:** | Pile Alle 3, 2000 Frederiksberg |
| **England and Wales:** | Goldhay Way, Orton Goldhay, Peterborough PE2 0GZ |
| **Finland:** | PL 160, 00211 Helsinki |
| **France:** | BP 186, 63204 Riom Cedex |
| **Hungary:** | Alagi tér. 13, 1151 Budapest |
| **India:** | Church of North India Bhavan, 16 Pandit Pant Marg, New Delhi 110 001 |
| **Ireland (Northern Area):** | 44 Ulsterville Avenue, Belfast BT9 7AQ |
| **Ireland (Southern Area):** | 5 St James Terrace, Clonskeagh Road, Dublin 6 |
| **Italy:** | Via della Repubblica 114, 10060 S Secondo Pin. (To) |
| **Netherlands:** | Kooikersdreef 626, 7328 BS Apeldoorn |
| **New Zealand:** | PO Box 10-227, Auckland 4 |
| **Norway:** | Viges veg 20, 3700 Skien |
| **Scotland:** | 11 Coates Crescent, Edinburgh EH3 7AL |
| **S Africa:** | PO Box 890527 Lyndhurst, 2106 Johannesburg |
| **Spain:** | Calle Bravo Murillo 85, 28003 Madrid |
| **Sweden:** | Järnvägsgatan 34, 703 62 Örebro |
| **Switzerland (French):** | Chemin de Réchoz, 1027 Lonay/VD |
| **Switzerland (German):** | Postfach 256, 4622 Egerkingen |
| **West Germany:** | Hellerweg 51, 7300 Esslingen/N |
| **Zambia:** | PO Box 31890, Lusaka |
| **Zimbabwe:** | PO Box BE200, Belvedere, Harare |